HEROES OF RACING

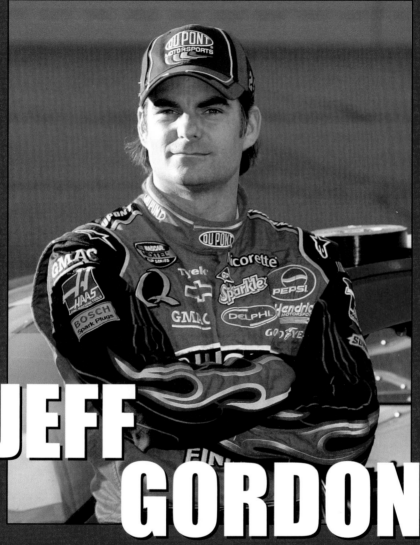

JEFF GORDON

Racing's Brightest Star

by Marty Gitlin

Enslow Publishers, Inc.
40 Industrial Road
Box 398
Berkeley Heights, NJ 07922
USA
http://www.enslow.com

Library of Congress Cataloging-in-Publication Data
Gitlin, Marty.
  Jeff Gordon : racing's brightest star / Marty Gitlin.
    p. cm. — (Heroes of racing)
  Summary: "A biography of NASCAR sports star Jeff Gordon"—Provided by publisher.
  Includes bibliographical references and index.
  ISBN-13: 978-0-7660-2997-2
  ISBN-10: 0-7660-2997-2
  1. Gordon, Jeff, 1971—Juvenile literature. 2. Stock car drivers—United States—Biography—Juvenile literature. I. Title.
  GV1032.G67G58 2008
  796.72092—dc22
  [B]

                            2007016055

Credits
Editorial Direction: Red Line Editorial (Bob Temple)
Editor: Sue Green
Designer: Becky Daum

Printed in the United States of America

10 9 8 7 6 5 4 3 2 1

To Our Readers: We have done our best to make sure all Internet addresses in this book were active and appropriate when we went to press. However, the author and the publisher have no control over and assume no liability for the material available on those Internet sites or on other Web sites they may link to. Any comments or suggestions can be sent by e-mail to comments@enslow.com or to the address on the back cover.

Disclaimer: This publication is not affiliated with, endorsed by, or sponsored by NASCAR. NASCAR®, WINSTON CUP®, NEXTEL CUP, BUSCH SERIES and CRAFTSMAN TRUCK SERIES are trademarks owned or controlled by the National Association for Stock Car Auto Racing, Inc., and are registered where indicated.

Photo credits: Jason Babyak/AP Images, 1; Mike Conroy/AP Images, 4; Chuck Burton/AP Images, 10, 93, 106; Dave Martin/AP Images, 12; Mike McCarn/AP Images, 16; Bettmann/Corbis, 26; Allsport/Getty Images, 31; AP Images, 34; Amy Sussman/AP Images, 39; Alan Marler/AP Images, 45; Robert Willett/AP Images, 50-51; Tim Russo/AP Images, 61; Paul Kizzle/AP Images, 65; Gerry Broome/AP Images, 67; Ed Bailey/AP Images, 68; Phil Coale/AP Images, 72-73; John Bazemore/AP Images, 74; Chuck Zoeller/AP Images, 78; Ric Feld/AP Images, 81; Chris O'Meara/AP Images, 82-83; Ben Margot/AP Images, 90; Eric Jamison/AP Images, 96-97; Larry Giberson/AP Images, 99; Darron Cummings, 104; Dima Gavrysh/AP Images, 110

Cover Photo: Jason Babyak/AP Images

CONTENTS

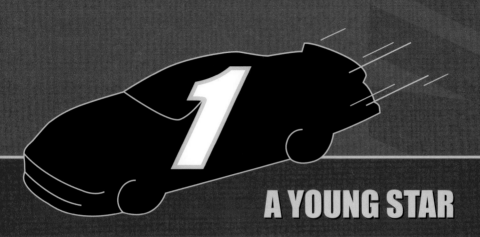

A YOUNG STAR

I t was February 11, 1993. The smiling young man waving in Victory Lane was twenty-one years old, but he could have been mistaken for a high school senior.

What was his name? It was Jeff Gordon.

Few even in the NASCAR world—and fewer among its growing legion of fans—were aware of the baby-faced kid with a tiny black peach-fuzz mustache. But there he was in all his glory, winner of the 125-mile (201-kilometer) qualifying race for the prestigious Daytona 500.

Jeff Gordon holds up his trophy after a 1994 win.

The youngest driver to ever win at the famed Daytona International Speedway soaked in the atmosphere, but suddenly his eyes met the stunningly beautiful model who was to present his trophy. Gordon winked at her. She winked back.

His personal life was about to change. His professional life was about to change. The balance of power in stock car racing was about to change.

NASCAR would never be the same.

The woman presenting the trophy was Brooke Sealey. In time, she would become Gordon's wife.

Their relationship played a role in his public perception as a "pretty boy" who would thrill some and anger others.

But such reaction to a man's image is not possible if the interest is not earned. His performance that afternoon in Florida was merely a preview to his later dominance. Gordon would soon establish himself as the premier driver in the world, a reputation he maintained throughout the decade.

DID YOU KNOW?

Brooke Sealey was born and raised in Winston-Salem, North Carolina. She attended the University of North Carolina and majored in psychology.

AN EARLY BLOOMER

Though a relative unknown before that Thursday afternoon in Daytona, Gordon had planted the seeds of racing success in the late 1980s. He became the youngest person to earn a license with the United States Auto Club at age 16. He won three sprint car track championships

DID YOU KNOW?

Gordon was featured for the first time on ESPN's Speedweek show at age thirteen.

before he was old enough to earn his driver's license.

Gordon was not satisfied with dominating and frustrating older American drivers. He ventured to Australia and New Zealand in the late 1980s to compete in sprint car races and was named the 1989 USAC Midget Rookie of the Year.

His passion for auto racing had been established early in life. The day of his graduation from Tri-West High School in Lizton, Indiana, he grabbed his diploma, traded his cap and gown for his racing gear, and high-tailed it to a dirt track race in nearby Bloomington that same night. By that time, Gordon had already won more than 100 races.

Many of his classmates were unaware of what their future would hold. Gordon was on a collision course with greatness.

His brilliance on the track was enhanced in 1990. The season after he was named USAC Midget Rookie of the Year, he became the youngest driver to win the Midget class championship. He was just nineteen.

The competition proved too easy for Gordon. He moved up to the USAC Silver Crown Division, in which the cars are similar, but larger, than Midgets and Sprints.

No problem. He won that championship as well.

AIMING FOR NASCAR

Despite his youth, Gordon decided to attend the Buck Baker driving school for aspiring NASCAR drivers. The moment Gordon stepped into his first stock car in June 1990 at the Rockingham Motor Speedway in North Carolina, it was love at first drive.

Gordon knew he had made the right decision to be a racecar driver as soon as he buckled himself into his seat at the driving school. The car was much bigger than anything he had driven before, but he loved it.

Now he needed a team owner to love him. But who would risk a few hundred thousand dollars on a kid, even one who sped past the competition throughout his young career?

The answer was nobody—yet.

DID YOU KNOW?

Buck Baker was an elite NASCAR driver in his own right. He won two Winston Cup championships and forty-six races. He opened his driving school in 1980.

It took some convincing, in the form of more championships. Late in 1990, Gordon raced in the Busch Grand National series, which is considered one step below the NASCAR circuit. He struggled at first, but he quickly became accustomed to stock car racing. He eventually won Rookie of the Year at that level for car owner Bill Davis in 1991 and earned about $100,000 in prize money.

That is when his relationship with crew chief and former driver Ray Evernham began to flourish. It was a duo that would wreak havoc in the racing world for several years.

Gordon and Evernham worked well together and had a lot of respect for each other. Gordon liked knowing that his crew chief had been a racecar driver. For Evernham to bring that experience to Gordon proved to be invaluable to the young driver.

Gordon knew exactly what he was doing, too. So did NASCAR car owner Rick Hendrick, who noted with amazement that Gordon captured a NASCAR-record eleven pole positions in 1992.

One day that year, Hendrick watched a driver race with what he considered reckless abandon around Atlanta Motor Speedway. With a sense of foreboding, he waited for a wreck. But a crash never occurred. Instead, that driver won the race. Hendrick asked an associate to identify the driver and was told, "It's that Gordon kid."[1]

Jeff Gordon shakes hands with Rick Hendrick at a news conference after announcing a long-term agreement in which Gordon became a part-owner of the Hendrick 24 team.

Soon thereafter, Hendrick instructed general manager Jimmy Johnson to sign "that Gordon kid" to a contract. Most young drivers are forced to get their feet wet with a mediocre team unwilling to risk a great deal of money on an inexperienced newcomer. Instead, Hendrick Motorsports threw caution to the wind and added Gordon to its stable.

It had not been an easy decision for Gordon, who felt a sense of loyalty to Davis. The car owner had been attempting to raise enough money from sponsors to form his own team, but his failure to do so made Gordon's decision clear.

NEW CHALLENGES

The theme of his first Winston Cup race in the 1992 Hooters 500 proved to be "Out with the old, in with the new." Gordon crashed and was forced to leave the race. More important, however, it marked legend Richard Petty's last race. The NASCAR landscape was about to be overhauled.

The race was not only Petty's farewell, it was the last race in the NASCAR series that year. By 1993, Gordon was ready. He proved his qualifier victory was no fluke by finishing a strong fifth in the Daytona 500. Though he had much to prove, the transformation in his professional life was complete. The transformation in his personal life was just beginning.

A rule barred drivers from dating Miss Winston women, but Gordon was falling in love with Sealey. They began their romance in secret. By 1994, they could hide no longer. The year after their eyes locked in Victory Lane at the Daytona International Speedway, they became husband and wife.

Meanwhile, Gordon was forced to deal with

DID YOU KNOW? When **Jeff Gordon won the 1993 Daytona 500 qualifier, he became the first rookie in thirty years to accomplish the feat.**

Gordon gives his fiancée, Brooke Sealy, a kiss after winning the 1994 Brickyard 400.

occasional failure on the track for the first time. His reputation as a reckless driver grew as he experienced mechanical breakdowns and accidents that knocked him out of several races. He barely escaped disaster in April when he spun backward into a wall and freed himself from his car before it burst into flames. During the summer, engine failure eliminated him from three consecutive events.

Sprinkled in with eleven top-ten performances his first year on the NASCAR circuit were eight finishes of thirtieth or lower and several blown leads. He was unaccustomed to such long races and placed in the top ten only twice in his last ten events.

Gordon, however, did take second in the Coca-Cola 600 and Miller 400 and third in the Champion 400. He also performed impressively enough to finish fourteenth in the overall standings in 1993 and earn yet another Rookie of the Year honor.

He was in the process of becoming a premier NASCAR driver. However, he also was more frequently a target of criticism for an image that many considered against the grain for its racing heroes. Some disliked him for his background and rapid rise. The sport had been dominated by southerners forced to scratch and claw to get to the top.

Critics felt Gordon had waltzed down the path of the privileged. He was born and raised in California, began his career in Indiana, and landed a spot at a young age on the prestigious and wealthy Hendrick team.

That, of course, was not his fault. After all, how could he feel shame or guilt for his upbringing and tremendous talent?

Just how did those factors result in Gordon developing into the most dominant and controversial racer in NASCAR?

To answer that question, we must travel back to the mid-1970s, when a preschool boy began his love affair with racing.

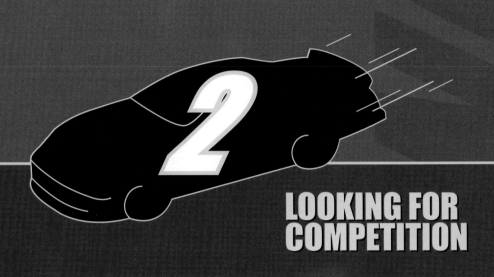

In a roundabout way, Jeff Gordon
was not old enough to roll over, let
alone toddle around, when his first
career move was made for him.

Gordon was a three-month-old
residing in Vallejo, California, when
his mother, Carol, and father, Will,
divorced. Jeff and his sister, Kim, were
living with their mother, who helped
support the family through her work
at a medical supply company.

In the summer of 1972, a fellow
employee and divorcee named John
Bickford summoned the courage to

ask Carol on a date. He also had a son and appreciated the importance Carol placed upon the well being of her children.

Bickford soon became a tremendous influence on Jeff's life. Carol developed a relationship with Bickford, who felt passionate about cars. He enjoyed taking them apart and putting them back together again. But most of all, he loved auto racing. In fact, he escorted the Gordon family to a Labor Day race at nearby Vallejo Speedway on his first date with Carol.

Jeff was still wearing diapers at the time, but his love affair with the sport could have been born that night. The love affair between John and Carol bloomed, too. They soon wed.

A BORN RACER

The bond between Bickford and Jeff strengthened just as quickly. Bickford's love for Jeff was equaled only by

THEY SAID IT

"Kids don't come out of the womb with their future occupation stamped on their foreheads. You're a product of your environment."

— John Bickford, Jeff Gordon's stepfather

Jeff Gordon poses with his stepfather, John Bickford, and mother, Carol Bickford, in Concord, North Carolina.

Jeff's respect for Bickford. When Jeff was three years old, Bickford taught him how to ride a two-wheel bicycle. Jeff skipped the tricycle stage altogether.

Their house had a hill near it, and Gordon would find anything with wheels on it to take on his thrill-seeking adventures down the hill. Riding a skateboard, bicycle or roller skates down the incline was just the start of Gordon's need for speed.

One day, he noticed neighborhood children scooting around on BMX racing bikes at a nearby track. Bickford purchased one for Jeff. Older kids soon got a taste of Jeff's natural talent and the feeling of losing to a younger driver. Adult professionals would eventually experience the same frustration.

"Mom said I looked like a baby out there, which wasn't far from the literal truth," Jeff said. "I was always a small kid, so when I was 4, I looked like a 2-year-old. I didn't care. The speed didn't bother me, and when I realized I was just as good as the older kids, I wanted to spend every spare minute racing. Winning was fun, even for a kid who could barely read the words on the trophies he was getting."[1]

Carol, however, became concerned her son would get into an accident riding his BMX. Bickford responded by purchasing a six-foot-long (two-meter-long) quarter midget car with a one-cylinder engine. Jeff was nervous about handling the steering wheel, gas pedal, and brakes, but that fear did not last long.

"I ran Rio Linda, Sunnyvale, Visalia, Pomona . . . mainly around the Sunnyvale-Fremont area, and Rio Linda, which was a dirt track we'd go to some weekends," he said. "In fact, the very first time I ever got into a racecar was at Rio Linda."[2]

Jeff's passion for racing had already been established. But his competitive fire began developing at age five, when he competed in quarter midget races against significantly older children. Others laughed at the sight of him racing around the track against kids sometimes more than twice his age.

Carol was not laughing. She became so upset at hearing her son teased, she convinced Bickford to adapt a midget car for her. Carol helped Jeff practice at the fairground. "We were always trying to prepare for the next opportunity—that would be the way to

DID YOU KNOW?

The midget car Gordon drove when he was five years old featured the name "Gordy" on its side.

say it," Bickford said. "I think all parents have a certain level of concern, but if he chose skydiving, I'd be more worried than racing."[3]

The chuckles turned to amazement when Jeff won his first race. He captured thirty-five main events. The following year, he was crowned Grand National Champion in Denver.

A star was born.

Nobody was laughing anymore. In fact, Gordon's dominance prompted fellow drivers to nickname John Bickford "the Roger Penske of Quarter Midgets" in reference to the dominant NASCAR racing team owner of his time.

A FEARLESS COMPETITOR

Jeff had already begun to develop the racing style that was to become his trademark. When spectators noticed the youngest driver in a race aggressively sprinting to the front of the pack with reckless abandon, they knew exactly who it was. He earned many black flags, which forced him to the sidelines for several laps, but it did not change his fearless approach.

Some critics refused to believe Jeff could be that talented at such a young age. They began whispering that Bickford was building cars that broke the rules. To prove them wrong, Bickford started selling his cars to the competition. The same drivers who finished well back in the pack before driving Bickford's creations performed no better after.

They were convinced. Jeff was that good. And he was proving it throughout the country. His parents traveled with him on weekends and during school vacations. Jeff sometimes flew back from races alone so he could attend school while his stepfather returned the family trailer back to California.

Soon Jeff had conquered that level of racing. He was performing well enough in school, but he had developed a one-track mind. His parents were fearful that quarter-midget racing no longer provided a challenge and that the jealousy of others would influence him negatively.

His next step would be go-karts.

CONTINUING DOMINANCE

If anyone thought Jeff would fail to dominate older competition driving 10-horsepower go-karts, they had another think coming. At age nine, he was humiliating those high school-aged drivers. In fact, he entered twenty-five speedway events in California that year and won them all.

The switch from quarter-midgets to go-karts brought bigger tracks and higher speeds. Jeff had to work harder, but he was still unbeatable.

It became apparent Jeff's talent, dedication, and passion created a formula others simply could not match. He could not find competition in go-kart or quarter-midget racing. When he won his second consecutive quarter-midget national title, it was obvious a new challenge had to be found.

Enter Superstock Lights. It did not matter, though. He began beating drivers as old as eighteen with regularity. Competitors began withdrawing from races they discovered Jeff had entered.

What made him so dominant? It was not just his love for the sport. He had also become a brilliant technician and tactician. While others nearly twice his age found it difficult to control their vehicles, Jeff always remained steady. He expertly passed fellow drivers and developed a sense of timing when it came to refueling.

DID YOU KNOW?

By the time Jeff Gordon was six years old, he had won thirty-five racing events and set several track records.

Jeff, however, was maturing faster as a driver than the levels of competition would normally allow for those his age. He was like a college quarterback playing against junior high school defenses. There was nothing more for him to prove. Bickford feared his stepson's skills would stagnate. He constantly sought new challenges.

There was nowhere to go but way up. And that was the sprint-car division. Was Jeff ready for cars with 650-horsepower engines that went from 0 to 60 miles per hour (0 to 97 kilometers per hour) in three seconds? Was he prepared to drive powerful machines that approached 140 mph (225 kph)? Would it be too dangerous for a pre-teen no matter how skilled? And who would allow Jeff to compete at such an age? He was still about three years away from getting his driver's license!

All those questions had to be answered. But first, Bickford asked an acquaintance named Lee Osbourne to build a sprint car.

Osbourne couldn't believe his ears. He knew Bickford loved racecars, but did he really want to drive a sprint car? Finally, Bickford explained that the car was not for himself, but for Jeff.

Osbourne was stunned. He was also apprehensive. He did not want to be responsible for a thirteen-year-old becoming seriously injured—or worse—in a powerful sprint car he had created. But when he laid eyes on Gordon racing a go-kart, he was impressed enough to go ahead with the project.

Where would the money to purchase a $40,000 sprint car come from?

"John was savvy," Jeff recalled. "Not only did he convince Lee Osbourne to build a chassis for us, he convinced him to do it on trade for racing parts that John manufactured in his shop. He then sold our boat and raised enough money to buy a used motor, which he assembled and installed. In one month, we went from having no car and no prospects, to being ready to go racing for under $10,000."[4]

One problem was solved. He had a sprint car, but he had no competition in which to drive it. He and Bickford searched the country for sprint-car races with no minimum age requirements. They found one in Jacksonville, Florida.

BUILDING HIS SKILLS

When Bickford and Jeff arrived in Florida, dumbfounded race officials attempted to convince them to go back to California. How could a thirteen-year-old compete in a sprint-car race and survive physically and emotionally, they asked?

This time, the fears were justified. The competition roared past him from the start. Rain pelted down on the pavement. Jeff nearly rammed into the wall, but he only grazed it before adjusting. He admitted later he was frightened.

Jeff was lucky. The race was cancelled due to the wet conditions. But rather than surrender to his fears, he entered another sprint-car race with no

DID YOU KNOW?

Jeff Gordon's first professional racing victory was in Tampa, Florida, and it earned him $300.

age restriction in Tampa a week later.

Those seven days allowed him to regroup mentally. He proved smart enough to race cautiously, feeling his way into the higher level of competition. Jeff remained in control throughout that race and following races. He no longer dominated as he did in quarter midgets and go-kart racing, but that was a positive development. The high quality of competition would raise his skill level.

TAKING ON HIS IDOL

One of the competitors in Jeff Gordon's first race after moving to Indiana was his boyhood idol, Steve Kinser, who made his name in the World of Outlaws series. Gordon nearly beat Kinser, who passed him on the final lap.

By the end of that short season, he was moving up in the standings. When Jeff returned to California, he had lost the desire to race anything but sprint cars. But until that season began in Florida, all he could do was practice and occasionally dominate the quarter midget and go-kart competition.

Jeff was getting bored. While millions of people were moving to California, he knew he had to get out.

NEW CHALLENGES IN A NEW STATE

By the time Jeff became a teenager, he no longer found racing in California enjoyable. He discovered satisfaction could only be attained through overcoming challenges. Lapping the field in local quarter-midget or go-kart competition did not provide any.

As with other teens, his focus also widened. He began thinking about girls. He began taking school more seriously. He sought new worlds to conquer. Jeff's parents started lightening his schedule. Upon returning to California, he began racing just once or twice a month. In the meantime, they attempted to broaden his horizons while maintaining his competitive spirit.

In the process, they discovered their son's talents were not limited to the track. Bickford taught him to water-ski and watched with amazement as he stayed afloat on just one ski in his first attempt. It was apparent he yearned to be the best no matter the endeavor. Jeff was so impressive when he took lessons that his instructors urged him to turn professional.

But Jeff had other ideas. He could not wait to return to Florida for another sprint-car racing season. Though he again failed to top the field in any event, he managed to work his way into the top five on occasion. He was earning admiration from his fellow drivers. But soon he was back in California.

DID YOU KNOW?

The Gordons did not own a farm in Pittsboro, Indiana, but it is considered mostly a farming community.

A BIG MOVE

It was the same old story. Something had to be done. Jeff had outgrown the world of local racing. If his career was to shift out of neutral, he had to move. By the time he was fourteen, his family had relocated to Pittsboro, Indiana, a fifteen-minute drive from the legendary Indianapolis Motor Speedway.

The Indianapolis Motor Speedway is home to the Indianapolis 500 each year.

"It was one of those crossroads in life you come to where you're going to have to make a commitment to something, whether it's your life or your kid's life," Bickford said. "And I felt the potential in our family lied in our ability to do what it took to advance the kid."[1]

Living and competing in the hotbed of Indy Car racing gave Jeff an additional career option. Because of the famous annual Indianapolis 500 race, that circuit remained more popular than NASCAR at the time.

The move was not without its drawbacks. Bickford had surrendered his small manufacturing business in California to maximize his son's professional possibilities. Money was tight. Bickford recalls those financial struggles when defending Jeff from those claiming his upbringing was superior to most NASCAR drivers because he was brought up in wealth.

"We slept in pick-up trucks and made our own parts," Bickford told *Newsweek* magazine. "That's why I think Jeff is misunderstood by people who think he was born to rich parents and had a silver spoon in his mouth."

Not only did moving to Indiana bring Jeff closer to the heartland of American auto racing, it allowed him to compete in sprint-car events most of the year. Indiana, as well as many other midwestern states, held no age restrictions on sprint-car drivers. Racing officials in the area figured requiring parental permission would be enough to keep fourteen-year-olds such as Jeff from entering.

But Jeff wasn't just any typical 14 year-old. He wanted to race sprint cars, and he wanted to race them now.

Getting the green flag to race from his parents was no problem. However, finding the money to maintain sprint cars that cost about $25,000 to build was an issue.

TOUGH TIMES

Bickford and Jeff moved to Indiana before the rest of the family to give Carol time to sell the house and Jeff's sister, Kim, time to finish the school year. Stepfather and stepson could not even afford to stay in motels during their travels from race to race.

Jeff's life proved difficult socially as well. While his friends at Tri-West High School hung out at malls and attended movies on weekends, Jeff often called in sick on Fridays with the understanding of school officials, and then took off in his stepfather's pick-up truck.

He did find time to date, run for the cross country team, and play the saxophone in attempting to maintain some kind of a normal life. But Jeff could not live as a typical teenager. He was driven to be a driver.

DID YOU KNOW?

Gordon's favorite class at Tri-West High School was science.

The same year he was old enough to get his standard driver's license, he was old enough to join the United States Auto Club, which sanctioned sprint-car races throughout the country. He did so when he turned sixteen, becoming the youngest driver ever registered with the organization.

Racing in the Midwest provided Jeff with a variety of tracks on which to compete. Some were paved. Others were dirt. Some races were for cars with wings, which help the vehicles stay down on the track. Others were for non-winged cars, which require a high skill level.

Jeff learned a great deal about his profession during that time. He was still highly successful, even against drivers more than twice his age. But the challenges of stiffer competition against more experienced talent not only improved his own skills, it strengthened his resolve. And he learned every step of the way.

WINNING WAYS

He captured his first sprint-car race victory in Chillicothe, Ohio, in 1986. He won two more before he even obtained his driver's license. He practiced religiously at the Bloomington (Indiana) Speedway, which he considered his home track. During the early stages of his sprint-car career, he performed better in pre-race qualifiers than in actual events, often earning pole positions. He raced well at Bloomington and then began winning competitions outside his comfort zone.

DID YOU KNOW? Gordon was voted Most Popular Boy in his class and was also chosen king of the senior prom.

Jeff understood it would take time. The jump in competition and required skill level from midget and go-kart racing to sprint cars was staggering.

But just a few years after leaving California behind, he was among the most respected drivers on the sprint-car circuit.

Prize money for sprint car drivers did not exactly make them rich. If he was to maximize his potential, Jeff needed financial backing. Before he graduated from high school, his talent caught the attention of Australian racing enthusiast John Rae, who would soon become his sponsor.

It was a risk for Rae. Sponsors only make money if their drivers win. Rae paid for Jeff's living expenses on the road and for the maintenance of his car. If Jeff did not perform well, Rae would not make money. Rae sent Jeff to Australia and New Zealand with the hope he would continue to progress.

PROVING HIS POTENTIAL

Jeff progressed, all right, beyond Rae's wildest dreams. Wide-eyed and relieved at his relative comfort financially, Jeff took those countries by storm. He not only won races, he set standards. In fifteen starts, he won fourteen races and established new track records in all of them.

Filled with confidence, Jeff returned to the United States and treated its competition the same way as he did in Australia and New Zealand. Just before his high school graduation, he won his first USAC race of the season in Kentucky, which kicked off a

Jeff Gordon checks out his car before the start of a race.

blistering run. Jeff sprinted to the top of the series standings with four victories and several other strong finishes. But he had enough trophies. He was no longer concerned with piling up victories. His focus was on furthering his career. Jeff had become intrigued with Indy Car racing. He geared himself toward that circuit by turning his attention to midget cars.

Though considered a step down from sprints, midget-car racing was a steppingstone to Indy Car racing. Jeff did not stumble over that step. He not only won his first USAC midget-car race, he set a track record. By the time that season was completed, Jeff had been named USAC Midget Rookie of the Year.

His dominance continued in the 1990 season, during which he won nine of twenty-one starts and captured the title. At the age of nineteen, he was the youngest national champion in the history of that circuit.

With success brought new and more difficult decisions. Should he continue on the path to the Indy Car circuit? Should he opt for Formula One, which are run on street courses in powerful open-wheeled cars and are held mostly in Europe? He was unaccustomed to such driving, which required speeds of 200 mph (322 kph) down straightaways and 30 mph (48 kph) on hairpin turns. Or should he race stock cars in NASCAR competition?

Jeff was now old enough to make up his own mind. He quickly discarded Formula One. But he was torn between the other two options. He needed to make a decision.

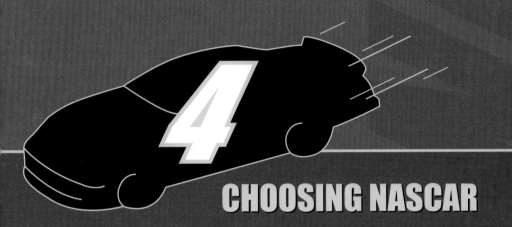

CHOOSING NASCAR

History was not on the side of NASCAR as Gordon considered his career options. The achievements of such legends as Mario Andretti, Al Unser, and A.J. Foyt peppered the Indy Car record books for generations. They were names revered in the auto-racing world.

Though Gordon had spent a relatively short time in Indiana, he had become a Hoosier from head to toe. The thought of racing in the famed Indianapolis 500 tempted him. And NASCAR had yet to be established as the most popular racing circuit in the

United States. Gordon even considered Formula One. His time in Australia and New Zealand had provided him a taste of world travel. Competing in Formula One would allow him to experience a professional and personal life outside the United States. It was an exciting thought.

Like Indy car driver Mario Andretti did in 1969, Gordon had always wanted to win the Indianapolis 500.

TOO FAST FOR MOM

Gordon took his mother for a special test drive during his time with the Buck Baker driving school. She told him to slow down when he reached 150 mph (241 kph).

Those were among the possibilities Gordon pondered in the summer of 1990. Suitors tugged at him from all sides. Among the most influential was Indianapolis Motor Speedway boss and eventual Indy Racing League founder Tony George, who attempted to lure Gordon into the famed Brickyard.

WEIGHING HIS OPTIONS

George lured Gordon with money and fame. He spoke of Gordon as the successor to the greats of American open-wheel car racing. Indy Car racing was rapidly losing prestige and popularity to NASCAR. George needed a savior, and he saw one in the form of the handsome, daring young driver from the Indiana heartland.

Gordon had become quite familiar with Indy Car racing. Bickford recommended he learn more about NASCAR by attending the Buck Baker driving school in Rockingham, North Carolina. Cable sports network ESPN, which had followed Gordon's incredible accomplishments as a teenager, took note. Baker taught Gordon free of charge in return for the publicity on the ESPN's *Thursday Night Thunder* show.

"Television promotion is so important in any sport, but especially to young guys in racing," said Gordon in 1991. "I don't know what would have happened without (ESPN). Last year was just an unbelievable year, and a lot of my wins happened to be on television.

"We used each other, though. I used ESPN to promote my career; they used me to promote *Thursday Night Thunder*. But it's like anything else; you (have to) use your assets."[1]

One lap around the track in a stock car was all Gordon needed. He wanted to be a NASCAR driver.

"It was the first time I'd raced anything that big, heavy and full-bodied," Gordon wrote in his autobiography. "The biggest thing I'd raced prior to that day was a sprint car that weighed about 1,400 pounds. Stock cars weigh 3,400 pounds. This was old-fashioned racing with big machines that had big rumbling engines and a lot of metal.

"This was also the first time I'd driven on a track with such high banking. In sprint cars and midgets, banking was non-existent. Rockingham had 23 degrees in turns three and four. Driving into the corners with that much banking was the smoothest, best-feeling ride I'd ever taken. After turning a few laps, I was home. I was 19 years old, and I knew what I wanted to do with my career."[2]

JEFF GORDON, NASCAR DRIVER

Car owner Hugh Connerty wanted Gordon to be a NASCAR driver as well. He was so impressed with Gordon's talent that he offered him an opportunity to drive his Pontiac in the 1990 AC Delco 200 Busch series event in Rockingham. When Gordon qualified for the race, his emotions burst forth.

"I'm so happy right now I'm about to cry," Gordon admitted. "I'm just having a hard time right now believing this is happening to me. I never dreamed I could do anything like this."[3]

Gordon was soon to be even happier. Connerty introduced Gordon to crew chief Ray Evernham, with whom he was immediately impressed. Gordon saw Evernham as a father figure, one who reminded him quite a bit of his stepfather.

DID YOU KNOW? Hugh Connerty Jr. is the president of the Outback Steakhouse restaurant chain.

As it turns out, Evernham was far more skeptical about Gordon than Gordon was about him.

"Ray was a show-me guy, just like my dad," Gordon said. "In fact, their personalities were so similar it was scary at times. Ray listened and asked a few questions. Then he decided to make a trip down to Charlotte to meet me.

"We hit it off right away, or at least I thought we did. In just a few minutes of speaking with Ray I had a great feeling about him. He reminded me of my dad, with different experiences and perspectives, but with the same drive and focus. I thought we had an instant chemistry."[4]

The feeling was not quite mutual. Evernham later wrote that he was concerned with Gordon's youth and inexperience. He would not be for long.

EARLY STRUGGLES

Gordon did not take the Busch series by storm. Though he qualified second for the AC Delco 200, he crashed thirty-three laps into that race and failed to qualify for the next two. He began to feel overwhelmed by the transition into Busch Grand National racing. It took quite a while for him to adjust to stock car racing, particularly at a level he had never experienced.

THEY SAID IT

"The very first time I saw Jeff, he looked about 14 or 15 years old. His mother was with him, and he had a briefcase in one hand. He called me Mr. Evernham. He was trying to grow a mustache, not very successfully, and when he opened his briefcase, he had a video game, a cell phone, and racing magazine in it. I asked myself, 'What am I getting myself into?'"

— Ray Evernham

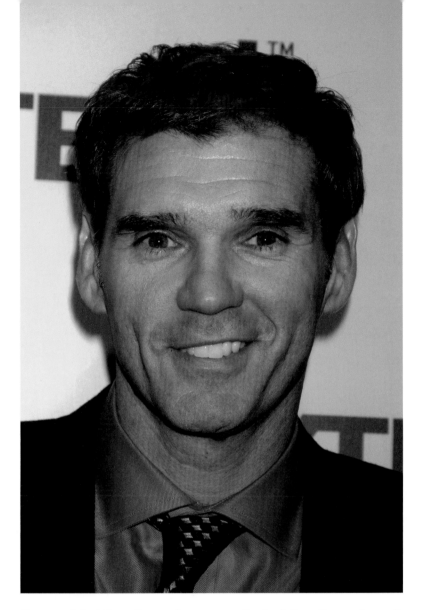

Crew chief Ray Evernham reminded Gordon a lot of his stepfather.

"This was the first car I'd ever driven where I was enclosed in a cockpit," Gordon explained. "Sure, the driver's window is open (covered by netting), but in midgets and sprinters I was fully exposed with only a roll cage surrounding me. The wheelbases are different, the balance is different, and the aerodynamics are different.

"There were times in sprint car, midget, and particularly in dirt car racing where I expected the rear end of the car to get loose in every turn. The rear wheels slid out from under you, and you over-steered to get back on line, sort of a controlled skid. When a Busch car gets away from you, you're probably going into the wall."[5]

His career was not going any better off the track. When Connerty failed to find a sponsor in 1990, Gordon feared his racing career was over. Bickford began burning up the phone lines to find an owner who would take a chance on a painfully young driver.

That is when fortune turned their way.

A STROKE OF LUCK

Mark Martin had been driving the Carolina Ford Dealers car owned by Bill Davis, but he left to form his own team. Davis offered that car to Gordon, who felt flattered.

The 1991 Busch Grand National series awaited. But one race the year before did not prepare Gordon for the rigors of a full season or the intricacies of stock car racing. He failed to qualify for the opening race, and then finished no higher than thirteenth in his next five. Gordon did not break through until finishing second in the Nestle 200 in April. When he began making progress, he did not stop until he was the premier NASCAR driver in America.

He did not experience the joy of crossing the finish line ahead of all his competition in 1991. But he won the pole position at Orange County Speedway in Rougemont, North Carolina, and finished in the top ten five times in an seven-race stretch. And when the tires had stopped squealing that season, Gordon had beaten out David Green for Rookie of the Year honors.

For Gordon to zoom his way to the top, however, it would take a premier crew chief. Evernham had been working for Alan Kulwicki in 1991 but quit at the end of the season. He bumped into Gordon, who needed about a half-second to ask Evernham about the possibility of joining his team.

DID YOU KNOW? Ray Evernham founded Evernham Motorsports in 1999 and helped Dodge return to NASCAR two years later.

"Of course, I was in no position to offer Ray a job, so I had a lot of selling to do," Gordon said. "After a couple intense conversations with (Davis), Ray joined our team for the 1992 season."[6]

Gordon earned enough money in 1991 to afford his own home in Charlotte. But he remained in close contact with his parents, seeking out their advice and

DID YOU KNOW?

An engine failure or accident knocked Gordon out of four of his last ten events as a 1991 Busch series rookie.

making certain they strongly favored any decisions he made. One decision about which he needed no guidance, however, was that of hiring Evernham as crew chief.

Gordon's belief that Evernham and Bickford would strike up a strong relationship came to be true. The two forged a friendship. But more important, Evernham helped Gordon as a technician and as a brutally honest coach.

By the time the 1992 season rolled around, Gordon had experience, a new sponsor in Baby Ruth, a dedicated team, and a tremendous crew chief. His career was about to take off.

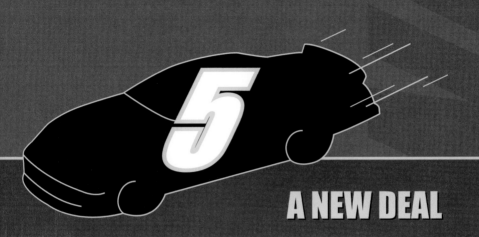

One March day in 1992, Winston Cup car owner Rick Hendrick noticed a driver careening around corners in a Busch series race at the Atlanta Motor Speedway. The car was being handled a bit more recklessly than Hendrick liked.

"You just can't drive a car that loose," Hendrick told those watching the race with him.[1]

The driver was Jeff Gordon. And on that fateful afternoon in Georgia, he won his first Busch series event. After a poor season-opening performance in the Goody's

300, Gordon began thriving at the highest level of racing he had experienced in his career. He won the pole position in his next three events, the last of which was in the Atlanta 300. He finished in the top ten in ten of his first fifteen races, including a visit to Victory Lane in the Champion 300.

The difference was not only Gordon's growing maturity as a driver, but the addition of Evernham, who earned the respect and admiration of the entire crew. When Evernham believed something needed to be achieved to maximize team success, it was considered done.

"Ray was a natural leader," Gordon said. "He had the command presence of a field general, and the motivating skills of a championship football coach. The crew had more of a spring in their steps when Ray was around.

"There wasn't a soul on our team who wouldn't work all night if Ray said that was what it took. Ray wouldn't ask anybody to do anything he wasn't ready, willing, and able to do himself, and nobody in the shop outworked him."[2]

AN UNBELIEVABLE OPPORTUNITY

Gordon had won over a new admirer that March day in Atlanta when he first experienced the thrill of crossing the finish line ahead of the competition to the cheers of a throng of fans who had risen to their feet. That admirer was Hendrick, who was overtaken by Gordon's youth, talent, and aggressiveness. The car owner admitted he was taken aback by Gordon's style and that the image of the young driver remained with him for days following the Atlanta 300.

He began considering Gordon a prime prospect for the Winston Cup (now known as the Nextel Cup), which is the highest level of NASCAR racing.

Jeff Gordon makes a pit stop during the Goodwrench Service 400 on February 23, 1997.

"All that day and the next day that image kept creeping into my brain," Hendrick said. "I couldn't get rid of it. I came back to the office in Charlotte and said to the manager of my motorsports division, 'I watched this kid, Gordon, and I hear he's only 19.' My manager said, 'Yeah, it's a shame he's got a contract.'

"A fellow named Andy Graves, who worked for me, just happened to be in the room at the time and said, 'He doesn't have a contract. I live with him. I'm his roommate. He has a one-year deal, and that's it.' When the kid said that, I figured this was one of those things that was just meant to be."[3]

Gordon's contract with Davis and Ford was indeed for just one year. He was quite satisfied with both. He knew Davis was working on a Winston Cup contract for the following year and was willing to follow him gladly. But he also left his options open in case Davis could not tie together a deal.

Considering his progress in the Busch series, Gordon believed he would be ready to take that final

RECORD SETTER
Gordon set a Busch series record by earning eleven pole positions during the 1992 season. He won three of those races.

step to the Winston Cup circuit in 1993. But when Graves told his roommate that Hendrick wanted him to call, Gordon thought he was joking. He ignored the message. If Gordon had believed one of the premier Winston Cup owners was interested in him, he would have raced to the phone.

DID YOU KNOW?

Gordon had a six-race stretch in his Busch series rookie year in which he finished no better than eleventh. Yet he still won Rookie of the Year.

When he did not hear from Gordon, Hendrick figured he had been snubbed.

Graves was caught in the middle, and he had to do something fast. He called Bickford and told him his son refused to believe Hendrick was interested. Bickford spoke with Hendrick directly then told his son he needed to follow through.

Gordon felt a commitment to Davis, but it was already May. Davis had yet to put a Winston Cup contract together. Hooking up with Hendrick meant switching from Ford to Chevy. It also might mean a new crew chief. That would never do. Gordon considered himself and Evernham a package deal.

When a car owner named Jack Roush expressed an interest in Gordon and spoke with Bickford, he was informed that Evernham had to be included. Roush replied that twenty-year-old drivers do not dictate who their Winston Cup crew chiefs will be. Bickford simply hung up the phone.

Hendrick, however, had an open mind. He wanted Gordon and also understood that Evernham had played a huge role in the young driver's success. In May 1992, Gordon was signed, sealed, and delivered to Hendrick. The folks at Ford were far from thrilled, but Gordon was becoming valued property. He simply could not make everyone happy.

And Hendrick felt as if he had beaten all his competitors to the punch.

"Nobody has ever tried to run a multi-car deal with a kid that age," Hendrick said. "Usually you've got a team and a sponsor lined up first, and the driver is one of the final components. I did exactly the opposite. I offered Jeff a job without having a sponsor, a team, or even a car for him.

"A lot of folks thought I was nuts, but I knew he had what it took. He had the looks, the personality, the skills, and Bickford had groomed him in a way that was far beyond his years. I figured I could get this incredible talent at a young age and mold him into a winning system. It was like getting a thoroughbred before anybody knows anything about him."[4]

DID YOU KNOW?

Jack Roush has been the car owner for such NASCAR driving standouts as Matt Kenseth, Mark Martin, and Kurt Busch.

Hendrick Motorsports had their thoroughbred for the 1993 season, but Gordon had a Busch series season to finish. And he also had some bad news for Davis, which he imparted to him on a flight to Charlotte.

"Bill didn't take it well," Gordon said. "He felt slighted, and I can't say I blame him. He was doing the best he could to put a sponsorship deal together so we could go Cup racing in 1993, but he didn't have any commitments.

"On the other hand, Rick didn't have a sponsor, either, but in his case, he didn't care. He was willing to offer me a generous contract and allow me to bring my own crew chief before he had a sponsor, a team, or a space carved out in his shop for us to work. I tried to explain my decision to Bill, but I wasn't very successful. From a business point of view it was a no-brainer. But Bill didn't see it has a business decision; he took it as a personal slight."[5]

FACING CRITICISM

His strained relationship with Davis the rest of that year did not help him on the track. Neither did the negative media attention he received for leaving Davis and Ford. But he would soon become accustomed to his share of public criticism.

Gordon suffered through an up-and-down season. He recovered to place in the top four in four

Crew members work on Jeff Gordon's car during a pit stop in the 1999 Dura-Lube/Big Kmart 400.

of the last nine races of the year, including another first-place finish in Charlotte. He hoped to win the Busch series championship for himself and for Davis. And in his second full year, he did finish fourth in the point standings.

He could not waste time on soothing his former owner's feelings. He was about to embark on a career in what was becoming the most prestigious racing circuit in the country. Soon thereafter he would become the biggest car-racing star in the United States.

DID YOU KNOW?

Bill Davis eventually worked his way up to Winston Cup ownership. He owns the car driven by Jeremy Mayfield, among others.

Jeff Gordon believed he had an understanding of the importance of a great team before he ever raced in a Winston Cup event. But the point was not driven home until he reached that elite level. Not until 1993 did he fully realize that, like any athlete in any sport, his success required a community effort.

He learned to appreciate that drivers did not make Winston Cup the premier circuit in the United States. Rather, their teams did. "As the season went along I discovered that the biggest difference between Winston Cup and the other series was parity," Gordon said. "The best Busch drivers were almost as good as the best Cup drivers, but the gap between the top Busch team and 30th-best Busch team was substantial.

"In Winston Cup, the difference between the top team and bottom team was minute. Every driver could drive. All the crew chiefs knew what they were doing. The crews were trained professionals, and there was only a fractional difference in the cars. That was a big change for me.

"By the latter half of the year I realized that I was going to lose a lot more than I was going to win at this level. I didn't have to like it, and I certainly didn't want to get used to it, but those were the facts of life."[1]

If Gordon was referring to "losing" as not finishing first, every driver loses most often. But eventually, he was to experience greater overall success than any NASCAR driver—just not yet.

A BIG ADJUSTMENT

After Gordon took the racing world by surprise, winning the Daytona 500 qualifier and placing a strong fifth in the main event, reality set in. Gordon managed sixth- and fourth-place finishes in two of his next three races, then experienced growing pains. He placed no higher than eighth in eight of his next nine events, the only exception being a strong second in the Coca-Cola 600.

Though he performed quite well in the longest race of the year, Gordon had not become familiar with the winning strategy in such marathons. He was accustomed to racing 200 or 300 miles (322 or 483 km). Now he was forced to double those lengths. It was draining physically, mentally, and emotionally. And maintaining such a high level of intensity at 190 mph (306 kph) for 500 (805 km) and even 600 miles (966 km) proved to be a tremendous adjustment.

In the process, he began dealing with both the negative and positive aspects of stardom. He experienced the thrill of seeing fans show up to events wearing clothing displaying his image and carrying Jeff Gordon posters and pictures they asked him to autograph. But he also received what he sometimes considered unfair criticism for his brash attitude and what was wrongly perceived as a privileged background.

Though his personal life had changed dramatically after he met his wife-to-be, Brooke, he had not lost focus professionally. He had come too far to be satisfied with just reaching the upper echelon of racing as a Winston Cup driver. He realized he had a great deal to learn as a rookie.

NEEDING DIRECTIONS

Gordon admits that after winning the 1993 Daytona 500 qualifier, he did not know where to find Victory Lane.

LEARNING ON A NEW LEVEL

It was not easy. Gordon had grown accustomed to winning week after week as a child and as a teenager. But the Busch series experience humbled him. Competing against the best in Winston Cup humbled him even more.

One problem was that Gordon had yet to understand how to temper his aggressive style on the track. Of the sixty races in which he competed his first two years, he failed to finish twenty-one, many because of wrecks.

"He doesn't use his car up," Evernham said. "He knows how to save it. But sometimes he puts his car in a position he shouldn't be in."[2]

DID YOU KNOW?

Dale Earnhardt won his seventh Winston Cup title in 1994. That tied him with Richard Petty for the most championships in NASCAR history.

Gordon, however, was too self-confident to allow mediocre performances to weaken his belief in himself. Midway through his first Winston Cup season he began to string together strong finishes. He placed second in the Miller 400, fifth in the Pepsi 400, and seventh in the Slick 50 300 in consecutive weeks. Though he slipped back in the pack the rest of the year, he finished fourteenth in overall points and was named Rookie of the Year.

The same night Gordon was presented with the trophy representing the top first-year driver during a ceremony in New York, Dale Earnhardt snagged the award for earning his sixth Winston Cup title and fifth in the last eight years. Earnhardt would soon receive competition from Gordon in the battle for NASCAR supremacy.

Though he understood visits to Victory Lane were going to be infrequent early in his career, Gordon regretted that he scored no wins in his first season. During the off-season he and Evernham mapped out a plan. With no fanfare, they set out to test various tracks to determine the best strategy for success on each. The pair spoke often about their desire to earn their first victory.

"I knew we were right on the cusp of doing something special, but we hadn't gotten there yet," Gordon said. "Until we did, we were just a young team with a lot of promise. Ray was a little more patient (the gap in our ages probably had something to do with that), but he was hungry. I could hear urgency in his voice."[3]

FOLLOW THE LEADER

Jeff Gordon led at some point in fourteen races during his rookie season of 1993 but did not win any of them. His longest stretch in the lead was eighty laps at Dover in mid-September.

At the beginning of the 1994 season, Evernham had posted a checklist in the garage. It read:

From Nobody to Upstart
From Upstart to Contender
From Contender to Winner
From Winner to Champion
From Champion to Dynasty

Evernham had already checked off the first two. In the next five years, the same could be said for all five.

IN THE WINNER'S CIRCLE

Early in 1994, however, Gordon questioned whether he had made any progress at all. He was still prone to accidents that prevented him from completing several events. He placed fourth in the season-opening Daytona 500 and in the top eight in two of the next three races before collapsing. Gordon finished no higher than fifteenth in the next six events.

He captured the pole position at the Coca-Cola 600 in Charlotte, his next scheduled race. He had finished a season-best second in that race in 1993. Though he had been struggling, perhaps he could perform well.

Nobody could have fathomed just how well Gordon would race that day. His car remained among the top five through the first 500 miles (805 km). A pit stop awaited all of them. The crew chiefs of the other drivers decided to err on the side of caution, changing all four tires.

"When I pulled down pit road," Gordon said, "Ray made the call that would change our day. 'Two tires,' he said. 'Right side only.'"[4]

The tire changes took his main competition eighteen seconds. His required ten seconds. Gordon left pit row with a 250-yard (229-meter) lead over Rusty Wallace and actually increased it. Evernham's gamble had paid off. Ray's voice on the radio was music to Gordon's ears:

"One (lap) to go. And you're pulling away."[5]

Tears welled up in Gordon's eyes, but he was able to finish the race. At the end, he was overcome with emotion. All his hard work had finally paid off in a victory on the NASCAR circuit in the racing hotbed of Charlotte. He expressed his joy from the winner's circle to the cheering crowd.

Others in his life felt his excitement. His mother and his girlfriend, Brooke, both watched his triumph on TV from a nearby condo. When his mother saw him crying, she cried as well.

Nothing could diminish the thrill he received from his first tour victory, but his next

DID YOU KNOW?

The 1994 Brickyard 400 at the Indianapolis Motor Speedway was the first NASCAR event held at that famed track, which had been used previously only for Indy Car racing.

A SMALL CELEBRATION
Jeff Gordon celebrated
his 1994 Brickyard 400
victory by ordering a
pizza and watching a tape
of the race with future
wife, Brooke Sealey.

one came close. Two months after the Coca-Cola 600, he returned home to Indianapolis to compete in the inaugural Brickyard 400. NASCAR was invading Indy Car territory with one of its hometown heroes.

Gordon played the conquering hero role before a throng of 350,000 fans at the famed Indianapolis Speedway. It was the largest crowd ever for a Winston Cup race. Gordon almost lost control of his car early when feuding brothers Geoff and Brett Bodine bumped, but he led for 93 of 160 laps. Most important, he led at the finish line.

Though he placed in the top ten six times in the final thirteen races of the 1994 season, Gordon knew he required fine-tuning to become a championship contender. He finished eighth in the overall point standings but failed to complete ten races that season due to mechanical difficulties or crashes.

So he and Evernham set out to fix those problems for 1995. They were successful beyond their wildest dreams.

Jeff Gordon celebrates after winning the Brickyard 400 on August 6, 1994.

7

THE COSTS OF SUCCESS

One fact had prevented Jeff Gordon from emerging as a championship contender in his first two Winston Cup seasons. You cannot win a race you do not finish.

Gordon had been doomed twenty-one times by wrecks and mechanical failure. His priority and that of his teammates in 1995 was to minimize such disasters. It appeared Gordon was capable of capturing a NASCAR title if he could simply complete all or nearly all of his races.

Gordon roared out of the gate in 1995, winning three of the first six events. Though two of his three "Did Not Finish" performances that season occurred in those first half-dozen races, he still won the Goodwrench 500, Purolator 500, and Food City 500.

That was merely a preview of the dominance to come.

Gordon finished in the top three in five straight events, struggled in late May and early June, and then established himself as the premier driver in NASCAR. He placed among the top eight in fourteen consecutive races from June 18 through October 1, winning the Pepsi 400, Slick 50 300, Mountain Dew Southern 500, and MBNA 500 along the way.

THEY SAID IT
"It's a shame. We had it, and we gave it away."

— Crew chief Ray Evernham after Gordon finished twenty-second in the 1995 Daytona 500

LEADER OF THE PACK
Gordon held the lead at some point in all but two races in 1995. He even finished third and fifth, respectively, in the events in which he never led.

The Slick 50 300 win in New Hampshire vaulted Gordon into first place in the point standings, a spot he was not to relinquish the rest of the year. At twenty-four years old, he became the youngest champion in NASCAR history.

The championship brought Gordon national fame. He was a guest on *The Late Show with David Letterman* and *Good Morning, America*. Supporters began trumpeting Gordon as a candidate to vault NASCAR interest beyond the South and hard-core fans elsewhere.

Most of America had yet to catch on to auto racing in general. It still lagged well behind major sports such as baseball, football, and basketball in popularity and TV ratings. Some believed a kid from California could push NASCAR into the mainstream.

"Can he do what (boxer) Muhammad Ali and (basketball player) Michael Jordan did and go beyond his sport?" asked Charlotte Motor Speedway president Humpy Wheeler in a *Fortune* magazine interview. "He might, because he's the antithesis of what a racer should be. He's not a good ol' tobacco-chewing guy.

"But he needs what Ali and (golfer Arnold Palmer) had—great victories against tremendous competition. Now, he makes it look too easy."[1]

Jeff Gordon poses with entertainer Britney Spears, who was the grand marshal for the Pepsi 400 in 2001.

DID YOU KNOW?

Jeff Gordon started in the pole position in only one of the seven races he won in 1995. He earned the pole nine times that year, winning only at Rockingham in those events.

A RIVALRY IS BORN

What was a positive on the surface became a negative to many. Some fans, officials, and opposing drivers resented his image as a privileged character, one Gordon never promoted. They believed NASCAR was supposed to be the domain of competitors toughened by the challenges of growing up in the rural South and who overcame hardships to become champions.

Gordon simply did not fit that image. And to further distance himself from the traditional NASCAR fan, his primary competitor did. Earnhardt, the man he barely edged out for the 1995 crown, fit that stereotype perfectly. A personal battle was created. It was a rivalry of image and of their perceived backgrounds.

"Of course I wanted to beat Dale, just like he wanted to beat me," Gordon said. "We were competitors. I raced him hard, and he raced me hard. That's how we made our livings. To assume that I ramped my driving up a notch when Dale was on my rear, or that he elevated his driving when I was behind him, is an insult to the other drivers. It also shows a lack of understanding about our sport.

"Even if I wanted to 'take it to another level,' I couldn't, because I didn't have another level. I gave it everything I had in every race I ran from the moment the track went green until the checkered flag fell. To say that I took it to another level when Dale and I were battling in a race or for a championship is to assume that I was giving something less than my best the rest of the time."[2]

But it was more than that.

Jeff Gordon signs autographs before practice at Lowe's Motor Speedway.

Rookie of the Year Jeff Gordon poses with 1993 Winston Cup champion Dale Earnhardt.

"Dale had built a loyal following by positioning himself as 'The Intimidator' and 'The Man in Black.'" Gordon said. "To his legion of fans he was the bad boy of racing. He was also trying to become the only man in history to win eight Winston Cup titles, breaking the record he shared with The King, Richard Petty.

"I guess a lot of fans took exception to a 23-year-old nudging The Intimidator out of first place, but who knows? They might have taken exception to that I was from California while most of the other drivers were from the South. Plus, I didn't smoke, didn't chew tobacco, didn't go deer hunting, and would rather dive with a school of fish than sit in a boat and catch them.

"The more I won, the more fans I attracted, and the more people pulled against me. A lot of people loved that I was a young guy with a new team. Others might have thought I was destroying the fabric of the sport. This is when the first ... signs came out and the boo birds tuned up again when I was introduced."[3]

Gordon also had other problems off the track. He was forced to keep his relationship with Sealey a secret because Winston Cup drivers were not allowed to date Winston employees. The couple ducked around corners or

THEY SAID IT
"Jeff is so young, I guess they'll have to serve milk instead of champagne at the banquet."

—Dale Earnhardt, referring to the annual postseason NASCAR bash in New York in which awards are presented remained apart in public until her Miss Winston Cup stint was completed.

Rumors even spread about Gordon. The more he won, the more polarizing he became. Race fans either loved him or hated him.

TEARING UP THE TRACK

Gordon certainly added fuel to the fire in 1996. Though a poor performance in Charlotte in early October allowed teammate Terry Labonte to wrest away the championship, he was the most consistently strong NASCAR driver that year. He failed to finish the Daytona 500 and Goodwrench 400 to open the season but went on a tremendous tear, placing in the top three in each of the next six races, including wins in the Pontiac Excitement 400, TranSouth Financial 400, and Food City 500.

From March 3 to September 29, Gordon finished among the top seven in every race he completed. The only exceptions were two crashes and an engine failure. He placed first on the circuit with ten wins, which doubled the number earned by second-place Rusty Wallace.

During one particularly brilliant late-summer run, Gordon registered four firsts and two seconds. That streak featured consecutive winning performances in the MBNA 500, Hanes 500, and Tyson Holly Farms 400.

Criticism of the NASCAR point system resulted. Labonte won the 1996 championship despite just two first-place and seven second-place finishes. But Gordon had given Evernham the opportunity to mark off yet another milestone on the checklist posted in the garage. Gordon had taken the step from winner to champion. All that remained was progressing from champion to establishing a dynasty.

WINNING WAYS

Gordon would begin to do that in 1997 by earning a win in the most prestigious race on the circuit and one in which he had performed horribly the previous two years.

That, of course, was the season-opening Daytona 500. Gordon promised that victory for car owner Rick Hendrick, who was at home in North Carolina fighting leukemia.

"Jeff told me last night, 'I'm gonna win this race. I'm gonna make you smile tomorrow.' And he did," Hendrick said.[4]

Even then, Gordon could not avoid criticism. His daring pass of Earnhardt into second place caused a crash that wrecked Earnhardt's car. But Gordon insisted that Earnhardt's reaction to the maneuver resulted in the crash. Another pileup on Lap 196 ended the race with Gordon and Hendrick teammates Labonte and Ricky Craven placing 1-2-3.

Jeff Gordon (24), Terry Labonte (5), and Ricky Craven (25) finish 1-2-3 in the 1997 Daytona 500.

Gordon followed that triumph with a win in the Goodwrench Service 400. And though his 1997 record was dotted with more poor finishes than the previous year, he earned his second championship with ten first-place performances, including one in his old state on a new track—the California 500.

When Gordon was hot, he was torrid. He placed fifth or higher in twenty-two of his twenty-three top ten finishes in 1997. His earnings that season nearly doubled that of second-place finisher Dale Jarrett. He took home more than $1 million alone for winning the Mountain Dew Southern 500 in Darlington, after which he praised his team.

"It takes key people to make things work, and to me, the Rainbow Warriors are the most important part of all of this," he said following the victory, referring to the crew that worked on his rainbow-designed car. "They are an awesome team and the ones who really make it happen. They believe in each other and do whatever it takes to win. That's quite a commitment, so I feel it's important for me to give back that same commitment."[5]

Gordon was on a roll. His team was on a roll. They were all prepared to roll into arguably the most dominating season in NASCAR history.

Jeff Gordon jumps in the air from the roof of his car after winning the Winston Cup championship in 1997.

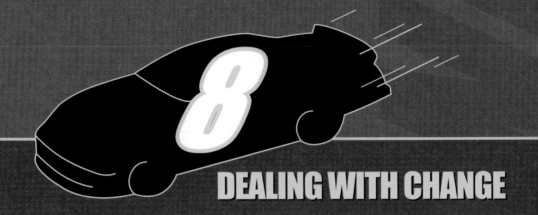

DEALING WITH CHANGE

It is one thing to set goals and quite another to achieve them.

When crew chief Ray Evernham posted a checklist in the garage in 1994 that highlighted "dynasty" as the ultimate aim, who would have believed such a lofty ambition was attainable?

Jeff Gordon did.

Four years later, Gordon drove his way into the record books. The 1998 season was an exercise in futility for his NASCAR competition, particularly from mid-June through November. Gordon went on an unprecedented roll, finishing in the top five in nineteen of the final twenty races of the season and top seven in all of them.

During that torrid stretch, he won ten races and placed in the top three in seventeen. A four-event winning streak during the heat of the summer included victories in the Pennsylvania 500, Brickyard 400, the Bud at the Glen, and Pepsi 400.

DID YOU KNOW? Gordon, who encountered problems finishing races early in his career, completed all but two events in both 1997 and 1998.

By the time the 1998 season had ended, Gordon had accomplished the following:

- Tied for third place for Winston Cup championships, behind only Earnhardt and Petty (seven apiece);
- Tied Petty for most wins in a season (13);
- Tied the modern-era NASCAR record with four consecutive victories;
- Became the first driver to earn more than $9 million in total earnings in a season;
- Compiled the most points (5,328) in NASCAR single-season history;

DID YOU KNOW? Gordon's string of six victories in seven events midway through the 1998 season is still considered one of the greatest stretches in NASCAR history.

Jeff Gordon stands next to his wife, Brooke, after winning the Pennsylvania 500 on July 26, 1998.

- Registered the most top-five finishes (26) in NASCAR single-season history;
- And became the first driver to win four straight Southern 500s.

A win in the SaveMart/Kragen 350 on June 28 gave Gordon the points lead in 1998, and he continued to pull away the rest of the season. And

ICING ON THE CAKE
Gordon had already clinched the 1998 Winston Cup championship before the final race in Atlanta. Yet he still won that event for his thirteenth victory of the season.

as he distanced himself from the competition, folks inside and outside NASCAR began thinking up reasons why he had become so dominant.

Many of them refused to list his immense talent as a primary factor. And he considered that an insult.

"A lot of people questioned the secret of our success," Gordon said. "Was it the cars? Did Hendrick Motorsports have the magic formula for building the perfect racecar? Was it Ray Evernham? Did he know something the rest of the crew chiefs didn't? Was it me? Did I have something the rest of the drivers didn't?

"I never answered any of those questions because I thought all of them missed the point. It was none of those things and all of those things. It was the team that made us what we were. Without Rick Hendrick's commitment and obsession to being the best in the business, nobody would be asking about our success because we wouldn't be winning. Without team members . . . we would not have been the envy of the Winston Cup garages."[1]

Some critics of Gordon theorized that Hendrick had come up with some futuristic way to cut down on resistance. Others called Evernham and his crew the best in the business. But relatively few credited Gordon.

One who did, however, was fellow driver Sterling Marlin.

Marlin saw what a lot of other drivers did not see. Instead of seeing Gordon as a pretty boy who walked into a big-money operation and benefited from Hendricks' knowledge and equipment, Marlin saw it the other way. He believes that Gordon's skill as a driver is what made the Hendricks team look good.

A NEW CHALLENGE

Prosperity, however, often encourages people to search for bigger challenges. The wildly successful 1998 season prompted Evernham to look into being a car owner. Late that year, he began feeling Gordon out about forming their own Busch racing team. PepsiCo, one of Gordon's long-time sponsors, had been seeking a stronger connection with the hottest driver in NASCAR, so a Busch car seemed to be an ideal outlet.

The details were ironed out quickly. Gordon would agree to race in six Busch events with young hopefuls such as Ricky Hendrick (Rick's son) driving the rest. Pepsi would sponsor the events in which Gordon raced, with the General Motors Automobile Company (GMAC) sponsoring the others. Evernham, Gordon, and his wife, Brooke, would own the car.

But Evernham remained antsy. He felt he had nothing more to prove as a crew chief after 1998 and began negotiating to start a new team with Dodge, which was looking to get back into NASCAR.

The 1999 season did not begin as if any distractions would prevent Gordon from remaining dominant. In the first three months, he won the Daytona 500,

Gordon holds the Winston Cup trophy over his head.

Pole sitter Jeff Gordon, front right, leads the way to the start of the Daytona 500 on February 14, 1999.

the Cracker Barrel 500, and the California 500. But the inconsistency and inability to finish races that haunted him early in his career reappeared. Crashes and mechanical failures prevented him from finishing four of his first thirteen events that year.

Gordon did place in the top four in nine of eleven races around midseason and won the NAPA AutoCare 500 and UAW-GM Quality 500 in successive weeks in October. But he ended the year placing tenth or lower in five consecutive events. After blowing away the field in 1998, he took just sixth overall in 1999.

CREW CHANGES

By the time Gordon slid into the driver's seat for the Exide Batteries 400 on September 11, he knew his crew chief was gone. Evernham had informed him the night before that he was taking the deal with Dodge and offered Gordon an opportunity to join him. But Gordon was loyal to Hendrick. Evernham had even asked John Bickford to join the team, but Gordon's father refused, saying he would rather remain friends than become partners.

A DIFFERENT KIND OF THRILL

Following the 1999 Daytona 500, Gordon and several other Winston Cup drivers went scuba diving in the Bahamas. Gordon still has a photo of himself with Rusty Wallace that was taken on the ocean floor.

"In a way, that summed up how I felt, too," Gordon said. "Ray and I had been friends, partners, team members, and champions. We had been to the top of the mountain together. Now it was time to go our separate ways. I was happy for Ray, and he said he was happy for me. I could tell he was excited about moving on. It was a great opportunity for him just as staying with Rick Hendrick was a great opportunity for me."[2]

Gordon finished a lowly fortieth the next day after transmission failure knocked him out of the race with ninety laps remaining. He then informed Hendrick that they had to find a new crew chief. That angered Evernham, who wished to give the car owner that news himself. Gordon apologized, but he explained that Hendrick needed to know as soon as possible so he could begin his search for a new crew chief.

They did not have to look far. They simply promoted Brian Whitesell, who had never expressed such an ambition but had served as team engineer during the three Winston Cup championship runs. Whitesell also had been named Western Auto's Mechanic of the Year in 1997. He appeared well qualified when Gordon won the two races in early October, but the chemistry that resulted in those three titles was gone. Much of the crew had left with Evernham.

Even Gordon's role would change. In October 1999, he bought an interest in the ownership of his team. He was not just the driver anymore. He was also a co-owner. And Whitesell did not remain crew chief for long. It was decided to make him team manager and look for a permanent replacement.

That was Robbie Loomis, who had worked for the legendary Richard Petty. Gordon was thrilled that Petty encouraged Loomis to take the position. To come highly recommended by a legend such as Petty meant a great deal to Gordon.

Gordon wrote in his autobiography that Petty told Loomis, "This is a good opportunity for you. Jeff's a winner. It wouldn't matter if he was playing golf or baseball or hockey or driving a racecar. Winners are gonna win, and they're gonna breed winners.

"You're looking for something that Jeff and I have already found. We've won races. We've won

YOUTH IS SERVED

When Gordon captured his third Winston Cup title in 1998, he was twenty-seven years old. Of the ten drivers who had won at least one of the ten titles previous to 1995, only Richard Petty was younger than twenty-eight.

THEY SAID IT

"He has supreme confidence in himself. He knows he has the potential to become the greatest driver ever."

— Jimmy Johnson, Hendrick Motorsports business manager

championships. That's what you're searching for. I've always told you that what you needed to find was a 25-year-old (actually 28-year-old) Richard Petty. I think you've got that in Jeff."[3]

Gordon was now a part-owner with a new crew chief. Chevrolet had instituted changes with the body style of his Monte Carlo. Goodyear had drastically changed the makeup of its racing tires and the 2000 season was fast approaching.

The new team needed to work quickly. And it was apparent through most of the 2000 season that they needed more time.

In sports, the term "rebuilding" means starting over. And rebuilding teams rarely contend for championships.

Jeff Gordon's team had a new crew chief—Robbie Loomis—in 2000. It had a new manager—Brian Whitesell—a new pit crew, a new car (a 2000 Monte Carlo), and new Goodyear tires. Many believed Gordon would struggle that year.

They were right.

"At the top level of any sport, the slightest change in the makeup of a team can have an adverse effect," Gordon said. "We had switched out almost every position. The people we had from the old team were in new jobs, and the new guys were still learning. People who expected us to come out and win a lot of races right off the bat either didn't know our sport or they were fooling themselves.

"At times in the first half of (2000), Robbie would look at Brian with a confused gaze in his eyes, and Brian would shrug his shoulders. The other team members saw this. They knew what was happening. This was a process. Every time we had a communications breakdown, even if the car was still running, it planted a seed of doubt."[1]

STRUGGLING

Gordon's misery translated into the joy of others. When an engine problem caused black smoke to billow from under his car at the Daytona 500, he heard the

BATTLING FOR STANDING

After winning the season-opening Daytona 500 in 1999, Jeff Gordon never held first place in the overall point standings that year. He never rose past fourth place after the fifth week of the season.

Gordon shares a laugh with crew chief Robbie Loomis after winning the 2000 Save Mart 350.

reaction from some fans. It hurt when they responded gleefully, and it hurt when he finally crossed the finish line in thirty-fourth place.

"Daytona was a tough day for me, and even tougher for Robbie," Gordon said. "When we went up in smoke, a throng of fans stood up and cheered. Later I heard Robbie say, 'Man, this is the worst day of my life, and we've got 200,000 people who think it's great!'"[2]

Gordon gave those 200,000 people and other critics more ammunition through late summer. He finished tenth or lower in fourteen of the first twenty-four events that season. Though he placed first in the DieHard 500 and SaveMart/Kragen 350, he could not find any consistency. More worrisome was that he deteriorated in August, placing no higher than twenty-third in any of the four races that month.

Some hinted that Evernham had been the key to Gordon's success. But Loomis believed the entire team, including Gordon, became a bit too conservative during the period of transition. Gordon and his team had thrived earlier in his career with an aggressive style and outlook.

Loomis did not want to propose radical changes, because he was new to Gordon's team and to the crew chief business. He also believed he had allowed his budding friendship with Gordon and Brooke to interfere with his ability to propose changes that might benefit the team at the track.

DID YOU KNOW?

Gordon's worst finish in a NASCAR event was a forty-third in Texas in the sixth week of the 1999 season. His car slammed into a wall, and he bruised his ribs. It was his first career-related injury.

"For the first two years, we had strictly a business relationship, but that evolved into a friendship as well," Loomis said. "And I was trying to be careful about that because I'm friends with both Jeff and Brooke. By the third or fourth month (in 2000) we got back around to mostly a business relationship because that's what we, as a team, needed."[3]

Gordon rebounded just as the 2000 season began to look like a complete disaster. He won only the Monte Carlo 400 during the last three months of that year, but he finished in the top nine in ten of the last eleven events. He even outscored 2000 Winston Cup champion Bobby Labonte during that stretch. The rebuilding appeared over. He and his team had hit their stride.

But could Gordon recapture the dominance and glory that resulted in three Winston Cup titles from 1995 to 1998? Could he refute the critics who claimed his success was the result of Evernham's brilliance rather than his own talent as a driver? Could Loomis prove he was a championship quality crew chief?

The answer to all those questions was "yes."

THE LOSS OF A LEGEND

The 2001 season began on a tragic note for auto racing when Dale Earnhardt was killed in a crash at the Daytona 500. Gordon had seen what he believed were far more severe wrecks than what had occurred that day. When he discovered that Earnhardt had not survived, he and the racing world were stunned.

"I watched the replays of the crash over and over to see if I had missed something," Gordon said. "I knew the car had taken a good lick, but no matter how many times I watched it, I kept saying to myself, 'There's no way that crash killed him.' Like everyone else, I was in shock.

"It would take days before the magnitude of what happened would sink in. We had lost a legend on

Tina Gray of Lincolnton, North Carolina, reads some of the words of sympathy on a card in front of Dale Earnhardt, Inc., headquarters in Mooresville, North Carolina.

the final lap of the biggest event of our season. In the days to come, my thoughts turned to the Earnhardt family. I couldn't imagine what they must be going through. Dale Jr. had finished second behind his teammate Michael Waltrip. Both those guys should have been celebrating with their owner. Instead, they were mourning his death.

"Then I thought about my feelings earlier that day, how I'd kicked the dirt in frustration and anger at being knocked out of the race with only 22 laps to go. It's things like losing Dale that make you think about how precious life is. You can't choose when you come into this world or when you leave it, so you need to live every minute as if it could be your last. The truth of life is, no one is promised tomorrow. And if something like this can happen to Dale Earnhardt, it can happen to any of us."[4]

Earnhardt's death cast a shadow over the entire NASCAR season, but it seemed to help inspire Gordon again to greatness. He finished in the top five in five of the next six events, including a victory in the UAW-DaimlerChrysler 400. Following two mediocre performances, he placed in the top three in six of the next seven races. His win in the MBNA Platinum 400 vaulted him atop the point standings.

Gordon followed that victory with another in the Kmart 400. He remained in first place overall for all but one week the rest of the year.

MORE TRAGEDY

A tragedy outside the sports realm halted the NASCAR season. On September 11, terrorists flew planes into American targets, including the World Trade Center, and killed thousands of people.

DID YOU KNOW? The garage used by legendary driver Dale Earnhardt was known on the circuit as the "Garage Mahal."

"I stayed home the rest of the week, thinking, watching, listening, and coming to grips with the new world and our role in it," Gordon said. "Racing was the last thing on my mind, other than to make a few resolutions. The word 'hero' had been thrown around a little too cavalierly in recent years. I'd been called a hero by some, as had plenty of other athletes.

"If September 11 did anything, it showed us what the true meaning of hero is, and it hammered home, once again, the fragility of life. I'd been reminded of that earlier in the year when we'd lost Dale. Now, everyone was reevaluating the meaning of life."[5]

Like other athletes, Gordon helped provide a diversion for Americans who needed one after the terrorist attacks. Despite placing no higher than sixth in the last eight events, he had secured his fourth Winston Cup title.

Gordon had not only proven himself a champion without Evernham, he had shown he could

Gordon drives the final lap of the UAW-DaimlerChrysler 400 at the Las Vegas Motor Speedway on March 4, 2001.

make a valuable contribution to his team outside his racecar. He had become more involved in making decisions regarding preparation of his car for events, including the aerodynamics package, chassis position, stiffness of shocks and springs, and air pressure in the

tires. "I think that I have had to grow up and mature quite a bit over the last few years," Gordon said. "Ray taught me a lot about being a driver and I have a lot to offer to the team because I have experienced a lot of things—wins, losses, and championships. I can offer confidence to the team and just keep the morale of the team always on the 'up' and go out there and focus on our jobs.

"To me, what makes a great racecar driver is someone that is able to be smart about the decisions being made on and off the racetrack, and not just the sheer bravery of it."[6]

Gordon had won his fourth crown, but the emergence of talented younger drivers and distractions in his personal life began taking a toll. He would remain one of the most successful in his field, but his run of dominance was over.

Jeff Gordon holds up his trophy after winning the Winston Cup championship in 2001.

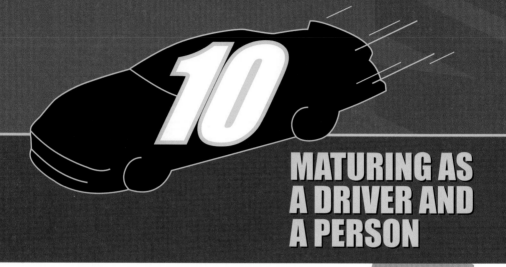

10 MATURING AS A DRIVER AND A PERSON

American couples get divorced every year in relative anonymity. But among the costs of celebrity is public scrutiny.

When Brooke filed for divorce from Jeff Gordon in 2002, the media no longer asked him about driving. The trashiest tabloid newspapers in the nation ran stories about the Gordons' crumbling relationship.

Jeff Gordon wanted to keep his personal life separate from his work, but it was impossible. He was peppered with questions from reporters, but he spoke little about his divorce. He attempted to prevent the situation from affecting his performance on the track.

His attempt failed.

PERSONAL PROBLEMS

Gordon's 2002 season was marked with inconsistency. He managed twenty top-ten finishes but placed fifteenth or lower in fourteen events. Not only was he distracted by the divorce and the resulting media attention, he might have spread himself too thin when he took on co-ownership along with Rick Hendrick of the Jimmie Johnson team.

That, however, was not the featured story in newspapers and sleazy tabloids throughout the country.

"Throughout the divorce I insisted it wasn't distracting me from my job as a racecar driver," Gordon said. "I tried to talk myself into believing that while I was going through it. It wasn't until after the (divorce) documents were signed and all matters were settled that I realized how wrong I had been.

"Whether it was the knowledge that I had to spend Monday morning with lawyers, or the thought of digging through a mountain of documents, the whole thing affected me more than I realized. I was still focused, and I think I did a great job of compartmentalizing, especially when I was in the car.

But in hindsight the divorce drained me, and it showed up in my 2002 performance."[1]

Former NASCAR driver Darrell Waltrip was one of many in the racing world who could sympathize.

"It had to (affect Gordon)," said Waltrip, a three-time NASCAR champion. "Jeff is a major celebrity and his and Brooke's divorce was splashed all over the headlines. He couldn't escape it. It's impossible for a driver to have to deal with all of that and at the same time remain focused on his job.

"I know when I was racing, I had to have everything exactly the same day after day, week after week. If there was the slightest difference—one of the kids was sick with the flu—it was a distraction. I can only imagine how tough it was for Jeff to try to keep his mind on racing while all of that mess was swirling around him."[2]

DID YOU KNOW?

Though Jeff Gordon finished fourth overall in 2002, he held leads in only fourteen races. That tied the lowest total of his career.

TRYING TO TURN THINGS AROUND

Gordon remained inconsistent throughout 2002, but he did perform better the last three months. He placed sixth or higher in eight of his last thirteen events, including a victory in the Protection One 400. He finished the year fourth in total points.

DOMINANCE IN MARTINSVILLE
Gordon earned the pole position only four times in 2003, but two of them were at Martinsville. He won both those events.

The influx of talent—due partially to the tremendous popularity NASCAR gained in recent years and the increase in prize money that resulted—made racing more challenging for Gordon and other veterans. Johnson was only one of many younger drivers who strengthened the field.

DOMINANCE IN MARTINSVILLE

Gordon earned the pole position only four times in 2003, but two of them were at Martinsville. He won both those events.

"That's probably what's changed most about our sport in recent years," Gordon said. "I mean, you not only have to fight hard every race, you have to fight hard every lap of every race. Six or seven years ago, you could save tires, save the car, cars would fall out and all you had to do was be there at the end . . . a lot has changed and it's tough to keep up with all of it all the time."[3]

Though his divorce was finalized in 2003, Gordon's performance on the track proved remarkably similar. He was inconsistent in the winter and spring, bottomed out in the summer, then rebounded late in the season. He placed out of the top ten in eight of nine races during the heat of the summer, then

Jeff Gordon stands next to the trophy he earned after winning the Brickyard 400 on August 8, 2004.

managed four consecutive fifth-place finishes before winning both the Subway 500 and MBNA 500.

Gordon earned three victories and took fourth in overall points in 2003. Some fans and media members began implying that Gordon was jealous of the success enjoyed by the new breed of NASCAR drivers, particularly teammate Jimmie Johnson.

Johnson, however, felt otherwise.

"I don't think that has Jeff miffed or that he thinks I'm even upstaging him," Johnson said. "He's a competitor and I'm a competitor. If you'll notice, during the race when it's time for give and take, both of us play that game pretty well together and give each other the breaks that are needed.

"When you get to the end of the race and have a million dollars on the line . . . both of us are going at each other as hard as we do anyone else. Would I turn Jeff around to have a position or would I rough him up? No. That's my teammate and I wouldn't do that to any of my teammates, but I'm going to race him as hard as I can."[4]

Gordon continued to race as hard as he could, but the results would not be the same. He did show flashes of his previous brilliance in 2004, winning five races. A masterful six-event run at midseason brought victories in the SaveMart 350, Pepsi 400, and Brickyard 400 sandwiched around three top-five finishes.

Parity, however, had become the norm in NAS-CAR. There were simply too many talented drivers for one to dominate as Gordon did in the late 1990s or Richard Petty did in

DID YOU KNOW? From July 3 to the end of the season in 2004, Gordon held on to first, second, or third place in the overall point standings.

previous years. In 2005, Gordon won three of the first nine events, including the Daytona 500. And after a second-place performance in the Dodge Charger 500, he was second overall and poised to make a run for a championship.

Gordon, however, collapsed. He placed thirtieth or lower in five of the next six events to fall to

TROUBLE ON THE TRACK
One reason for Jeff Gordon's eleventh-place finish in 2005 was that accidents and engine problems knocked him out of nine races.

fourteenth overall. He never fully recovered, though he did finish in the top ten in four of the last five races of the 2005 season. And in 2006, it took a second-half surge kicked off by victories in the SaveMart 350 and USG Sheetrock 400 for Gordon to place sixth overall.

A NEAR-MISS IN 2007

In 2007, Gordon returned to dominance not seen since his record-setting 1998 season. He won six races and finished in the top ten a career-high thirty times in thirty-six starts to set a NASCAR record.

Gordon (right) congratulates Jimmie Johnson after Johnson won the all-star race on May 17, 2003.

Cup championship number five appeared well within reach after Gordon won the Bank of America 500 on Oct. 13. But Johnson reeled off two victories in a row to set the stage for a memorable race for the Chase title.

With three races remaining in the Chase, Gordon led Johnson by nine points. At the Dickies 500 at Texas Motor Speedway, however, Gordon placed seventh and Johnson won the race to take a thirty-point lead. Johnson and Gordon then finished one-two in Phoenix, leaving Gordon a virtually insurmountable eighty-six points behind.

Gordon was unable to overcome the deficit in the finale at the Ford 400 at Homestead, Florida. He finished second in the final Cup standings, seventy-seven points behind the champion.

Gordon won his first race of the season at the Subway Fresh Fit 500 at Phoenix in the eighth race of the year. It was the first of four consecutive races Gordon started from the pole position. Gordon led from start to finish for the second week in a row to capture the Aaron's 499 at Talladega. He started from the pole at Richmond in the tenth race, and won the eleventh race-the Dodge Avenger 500 at Darlington.

Gordon didn't let up in the Chase, winning twice in the final ten races of the season. He finished in the top ten in nine of the Chase's ten races and was in the top six five times. In fact, he finished higher than

Johnson in 22 of the 36 races. But he only averaged eighth place in the final three races of the season, and that proved to be his undoing.

"You're so appreciative. You work so hard, and you really just never know when it's going to happen again. And that, to me, is the toughest part about this year for me personally," Gordon said following the final race. "I'm not getting any younger. I put up about as good a numbers as I know how to put up, and it wasn't enough. And that's tough to handle as a competitor."[5]

Still, Gordon's showing in 2007 proved that he remained among racing's giants.

GROWING AS A PERSON

A man should not be judged merely by professional accomplishments. Though the dominance that marked his earlier career was gone, he had grown mentally and emotionally. He began to seek out personal happiness and fulfillment. When he was king of the mountain in the racing world, his life behind the wheel defined him. By the time he reached his early thirties, he realized there was more to life than racing.

Perhaps it took his divorce to fully understand that, but those close to Gordon have seen the changes.

"We're seeing a new Jeff," said *Charlotte Observer* veteran motorsports writer David Poole. "He's now

Jeff Gordon and his wife, Ingrid Vandebosch, arrive at the Nextel Cup awards in 2006.

less guarded, more open with people. The single biggest change I see in Jeff is that—maybe for the first time in his life—he is doing things in a way he thinks is best for him. It used to be that he did everything to try to please other people.

"I don't know that his personality has changed. Jeff was never the type of guy to tell someone to get the (heck) away from him, and he's still a nice guy. He's still very personable and easy to get along with. He's still a great guy, but when someone goes through major changes in his life the way he has in the past year or so, he can't help but be affected."[6]

Gordon is no less competitive than when he was dominating NASCAR in the mid-to-late 1990s, but he is looking long-range at both his career and his life. "I'm no longer the 'Wonderboy' of (NASCAR)," Gordon said. "A lot of young guns are on the track today, and while I'm not the old man of the crowd, I have to work a lot harder to stay competitive with all the new, young drivers.

"I love that part of the sport, too. If my experience has shown me anything, it's that good people can rise to meet any challenge."[7]

It is not that Gordon has necessarily run more bad races in the last few years. It is that there are more talented drivers around to run good ones.

Although records are meant to be broken, nobody can take away the accomplishments that turned heads and turned America on to NASCAR. Gordon was arguably more responsible for the blossoming popularity of his sport than any racecar driver in history.

CAREER STATISTICS

Year	Rank	Starts	Wins	Poles
2007	2	36	6	7
2006	6	36	2	2
2005	11	36	4	2
2004	3	36	5	6
2003	4	36	3	4
2002	4	36	3	3
2001	1	36	6	6
2000	9	34	3	3

Top 5	Top 10	Earnings	Points
21	30	$7,148,620	6,646
14	18	$5,975,870	6,256
8	14	$6,855,440	4,174
16	25	$6,437,660	6,490
15	20	$5,107,760	4,785
13	20	$4,981,170	4,607
18	24	$6,649,080	5,112
11	22	$2,703,590	4,361

CAREER STATISTICS

Year	Rank	Starts	Wins	Poles
1999	6	34	7	7
1998	1	33	13	7
1997	1	32	10	1
1996	2	31	10	5
1995	1	31	7	8
1994	8	31	2	1
1993	14	30	0	1
1992	79	1	0	0

Top 5	Top 10	Earnings	Points
18	21	$5,281,361	4,620
26	28	$6,175,867	5,328
22	23	$4,201,227	4,710
21	24	$3,428,485	4,620
17	23	$2,088,460	4,614
7	14	$1,507,010	3,776
7	11	$623,855	3,447
0	0	$6,285	70

CAREER ACHIEVEMENTS

- Four-time Nextel/Winston Cup champion (1995, 1997, 1998, 2001)

- Three-time Daytona 500 winner (1997, 1999, 2005)

- Became third NASCAR driver to win four season championships (2001)

- Became youngest Winston Cup driver to achieve fifty victories (2000)

- Became first driver in Winston Cup history to exceed $4 million in single-season earnings (1997)

- At twenty-four years old, became youngest Winston Cup champion in history (1995)

FOR MORE INFORMATION

WEB LINKS

The official site of Hendrick Motorsports:
www.hendrickmotorsports.com

The official site of NASCAR:
www.nascar.com

The site of Jeff Gordon's charitable foundation:
www.jeffgordonfoundation.org

The site of the Jeff Gordon Racing School:
www.jeffgordonracingschool.com

FURTHER READING

Christopher, Matt. *On the Track with Jeff Gordon.* Boston: Little, Brown and Company, 2000.

Gordon, Jeff. *Jeff Gordon: Portrait of a Champion.* New York: HarperHorizon, 1998.

Gordon, Jeff, with Steve Eubanks. *Jeff Gordon: Racing Back to the Front, My Memoir.* New York: Atria Books, 2003.

Regruth, John. *Jeff Gordon.* St. Paul, Minn.: MBI Publishing Company, 2001.

Tiedemann, George. *Trading Paint: Dale Earnhardt vs. Jeff Gordon.* Kingston, N.Y.: Total/Sports Illustrated, 2001.

CHAPTER NOTES

CHAPTER 1. A YOUNG STAR

1. Busch series Statistics, *1992 Major Moves: Season Recap*, <www.gordonline.com/busch/bgn92.html> (February 2, 2007).

CHAPTER 2. LOOKING FOR COMPETITION

1. Jeff Gordon with Steve Eubanks, *Jeff Gordon: Racing Back to the Front, My Memoir*, New York: Atria Books, 2003, p. 20.
2. Biographical information, <www.gordonline.com/bio.html> (February 2, 2007).
3. Ibid.
4. Jeff Gordon with Steve Eubanks, *Jeff Gordon: Racing Back to the Front, My Memoir*, New York: Atria Books, 2003, p. 29.

CHAPTER 3. NEW CHALLENGES IN A NEW STATE

1. Biographical information, <www.gordonline.com/bio.html> (February 2, 2007).

CHAPTER 4. CHOOSING NASCAR

1. George Tiedemann, *Trading Paint: Dale Earnhardt vs. Jeff Gordon*, New York: Total Sports Illustrated, 2001, p. 24.
2. Jeff Gordon with Steve Eubanks, *Jeff Gordon: Racing Back to the Front, My Memoir*, New York: Atria Books, 2003, p. 43.
3. George Tiedemann, *Trading Paint: Dale Earnhardt vs. Jeff Gordon*, New York: Total Sports Illustrated, 2001, p. 26.
4. Jeff Gordon with Steve Eubanks, *Jeff Gordon: Racing Back to the Front, My Memoir*, New York: Atria Books, 2003, p. 47.
5. Ibid., p. 52.
6. Ibid., p. 56.

CHAPTER 5. A NEW DEAL

1. George Tiedemann, *Trading Paint: Dale Earnhardt vs. Jeff Gordon*, New York: Total Sports Illustrated, 2001, p. 57.

2. Jeff Gordon with Steve Eubanks, J*eff Gordon: Racing Back to the Front, My Memoir*, New York: Atria Books, 2003, p. 57.

3. Ibid., p. 59.

4. Ibid., p. 55.

5. Ibid., p. 57.

CHAPTER 6. LEARNING TO WIN ON THE NASCAR CIRCUIT

1. Jeff Gordon with Steve Eubanks, *Jeff Gordon: Racing Back to the Front, My Memoir*, New York: Atria Books, 2003, p. 83.

2. George Tiedemann, *Trading Paint: Dale Earnhardt vs. Jeff Gordon*, New York: Total Sports Illustrated, 2001, p. 34.

3. Jeff Gordon with Steve Eubanks, *Jeff Gordon: Racing Back to the Front, My Memoir*, New York: Atria Books, 2003, p. 84.

4. Ibid., p. 88.

5. Ibid.

CHAPTER 7. THE COSTS OF SUCCESS

1. John Regruth, *Jeff Gordon*, Walla Walla, Wash.: MBA Publishing Company, 2001, p. 43.

2. Jeff Gordon with Steve Eubanks, *Jeff Gordon: Racing Back to the Front, My Memoir*, New York: Atria Books, 2003, p. 94.

3. Ibid., p. 95.

4. Mark Aumann, *1997 Daytona 500: Youngest Winner Ever*, February, 10, 2003, <http://www.nascar.com/2003/kyn/history/daytona/02/10/daytona_1997/index.html> (February 2 2007).

5. Jeff Gordon, *Portrait of a Champion*, New York: HarperHorizon, 1998, p. 75.

CHAPTER 8. DEALING WITH CHANGE

1. Jeff Gordon with Steve Eubanks, *Jeff Gordon: Racing Back to the Front, My Memoir*, New York: Atria Books, 2003, p. 103.
2. Ibid., p. 124.
3. Ibid., p. 144.

CHAPTER 9. FACING ADVERSITY

1. Jeff Gordon with Steve Eubanks, J*eff Gordon: Racing Back to the Front, My Memoir*, New York: Atria Books, 2003, p. 160.
2. Ibid., p. 155.
3. Thomas Pope, Still the Man to Beat, *stockcarracing.com*, March 2004, <http://www.stockcarracing/thehistoryof/bio/134_0304_jeff_gordon_biography> (February 2, 2007).
4. Jeff Gordon with Steve Eubanks, *Jeff Gordon: Racing Back to the Front, My Memoir*, New York: Atria Books, 2003, p. 187.
5. Ibid., p. 205.
6. Chat Transcript: Jeff Gordon, *nascar.com*, August 8, 2001, <http://www.nascar.com/2001/NEWS/08/08/jgordon_transcript/index.html> (February 2, 2007).

CHAPTER 10. MATURING AS A DRIVER AND A PERSON

1. Jeff Gordon with Steve Eubanks, *Jeff Gordon: Racing Back to the Front, My Memoir*, New York: Atria Books, 2003, p. 112.

2. Larry Woody, From choir boy to playboy: Footloose and fancy-free, Jeff Gordon eschewing his squeaky-clean image and coming out of his cocoon, *Auto Racing Digest*, December 2003.

3. Thomas Pope, Still the Man to Beat, *stockcarracing.com*, March 2004, <http://www.stockcarracing/thehistoryof/bio/134_0304_jeff_gordon_biography> (February 2, 2007).

4. Ron LeMasters, *A Desert Rat's Race to NASCAR Stardom*, New York: Motorbooks International, 2004, p. 129.

5. Tom McCarthy, "Gordon's 2007 sets new standard of measurement," *nascar.com*, November 19, 2007, <http://www.nascar.com/2007/news/opinion/11/19/jgordon.runner.up.standard/index.html> (November 20, 2007)

6. Larry Woody, From choir boy to playboy: Footloose and fancy-free, Jeff Gordon eschewing his squeaky-clean image and coming out of his cocoon, *Auto Racing Digest*, December 2003.

7. Jeff Gordon with Steve Eubanks, *Jeff Gordon: Racing Back to the Front, My Memoir*, New York: Atria Books, 2003, p. 221.

GLOSSARY

aerodynamics—Airflow over and under the body and grill of the car and vacuum of turbulent air formed behind a car traveling at high speeds.

black flag—A flag waved at a particular car for a penalty or mechanical problem signaling the car in question must leave the track.

Busch series—A NASCAR circuit featuring slightly lighter and less powerful cars with events generally run the day before Winston Cup (now Nextel Cup) races.

chassis—The frame of a car.

crew chief—The manager of a race team who oversees the mechanics of the car and the crew and is responsible for its performance on race day.

driver—The team member behind the wheel of the car on race day.

lap—One trip around a track.

midget car—An open-wheel, 600-horsepower car most often raced on dirt tracks.

NASCAR—The National Association for Stock Car Auto Racing, which governs the Nextel Cup, formerly the Winston Cup series.

pit stop—Leaving the racetrack for service.

quarter midget—Open-wheeled cars with one-fourth the size and power of a midget car, generally for younger competitors.

red flag—The flag that stops all drivers in a race, most often due to wrecks and bad weather.

Rookie of the Year—The award given to the first-year NASCAR driver with the best fifteen finishes.

setup—The complete preparation of a car for a race.

sponsor—A corporation that pays to have its logos and identity associated with a particular race team.

team—All employees and staff of an organization assigned to a particular car.

Victory Lane—A section of the track infield in which the winning car and team celebrate.

INDEX

A

AC Delco 200, 37
Andretti, Mario, 33
Atlanta Motor Speedway, 9, 43
Atlanta 300, 44-45

B

Baby Ruth, 42
banking, 36
Bickford, Carol, 14, 15, 17, 28, 35, 59
Bickford, John, 14-19, 20, 21-22, 25, 26-27, 28, 35, 40, 42, 47-
    48, 84
Bloomington Speedway, 7, 29
Bodine, Brett, 60
Bodine, Geoff, 60
Brickyard 400, 59, 60, 77, 105
Bud at the Glen, 77

C

California 500, 75, 84
Carolina Ford Dealers, 40
Champion 300, 44
Champion 400, 13
Chase for the Cup, 45, 108
Coca-Cola 600, 13, 54, 58, 60
Connerty, Hugh, 37, 40
Cracker Barrel 500, 84
Craven, Ricky, 71